# AUBURN TIGERS

BY BRIAN HOWELL

Published by ABDO Publishing Company, PO Box 398166, Minneapolis, MN 55439. Copyright © 2013 by Abdo Consulting Group, Inc. International copyrights reserved in all countries. No part of this book may be reproduced in any form without written permission from the publisher. SportsZone™ is a trademark and logo of ABDO Publishing Company.

Printed in the United States of America,
North Mankato, Minnesota
052012
092012

THIS BOOK CONTAINS AT LEAST 10% RECYCLED MATERIALS.

Editor: Chrös McDougall
Series Designer: Craig Hinton

**Photo Credits:** Dave Martin/AP Images, cover, 15, 17; Collegiate Images/Getty Images, 1; Rick Scuteri/AP Images, 4, 9; Mark J. Terrill/AP Images, 6; Andre Jenny/Alamy, 10, 42 (top); Paul Abell/AP Images, 13; AP Images, 18, 35, 43 (top); Marvin E. Newman/Sports Illustrated/Getty Images, 23; Anthony Camerano/AP Images, 25, 42 (bottom left); Bill Haber/AP Images, 26; John Iacono/Sports Illustrated/Getty Images, 29, 42 (bottom right); Jerry Wachter/Sports Illustrated/Getty Images, 31; David Mills/AP Images, 32; John Amos/AP Images, 37, 43 (bottom left); John Bazemore/AP Images, 39; Matt York/AP Images, 41, 43 (bottom right); Kevin C. Cox/Getty Images, 44

**Library of Congress Cataloging-in-Publication Data**
Howell, Brian, 1974-
 Auburn Tigers / by Brian Howell.
   p. cm. -- (Inside college football)
 Includes index.
 ISBN 978-1-61783-495-0
 1. Auburn University--Football--History--Juvenile literature. 2. Auburn Tigers (Football team)--History--Juvenile literature. I. Title.
 GV958.A92H69 2013
 796.332'630976155--dc23

2012001848

# TABLE OF CONTENTS

1. TIGERS RISE TO THE TOP ....... 5
2. EARLY YEARS ............................. 11
3. NATIONAL CHAMPS ................. 19
4. DYE YEARS ................................. 27
5. WINNING TRADITION ............... 33

TIMELINE 42
QUICK STATS 44
QUOTES & ANECDOTES 45
GLOSSARY 46
FOR MORE INFORMATION 47
INDEX 48
ABOUT THE AUTHOR 48

Auburn running back Michael Dyer finds open field during the 2011 BCS National Championship Game against Oregon.

# TIGERS RISE TO THE TOP

**F**RESHMAN RUNNING BACK MICHAEL DYER WAS NOT THE BIGGEST STAR ON AUBURN UNIVERSITY'S FOOTBALL TEAM IN 2010. BUT ON THE NIGHT OF THE TIGERS' BIGGEST GAME OF THE YEAR, DYER SHINED.

On January 10, 2011, Auburn played Oregon in the Bowl Championship Series (BCS) National Championship Game. Auburn and Oregon were tied 19–19 with a little more than two minutes left in the game. Auburn needed some big plays to beat the Ducks. That is when Dyer stepped in.

Auburn was 60 yards from the end zone when star junior quarterback Cam Newton handed the ball to Dyer. Six yards later, Dyer appeared to be tackled by an Oregon defender. But Dyer's knee never touched the ground. And the referees never blew their whistles to stop the play. So after he stopped for a brief second, Dyer again took off running. He gained 37 yards on the play.

Auburn quarterback Cam Newton celebrates with fans after the Tigers won the 2011 BCS Championship Game.

"All I knew was the whistle wasn't blowing and my coach was saying 'Go!'" Dyer said.

Three plays later, Dyer again got the ball. This time, he ran 16 yards to the Oregon 1-yard line. Only 10 seconds remained in the game. Newton was stopped on the next play. But then Auburn kicker Wes Byrum drilled a 19-yard field goal as time expired. Dyer's running and Byrum's kick led Auburn to a 22–19 victory and the school's first national championship since 1957.

The Tigers had produced many great moments from 1958 to 2009. During that time, two Tigers won the Heisman Trophy, which is given to the best player in college football each year. The Tigers also had

[ 6 ]

three undefeated seasons during that time. And they had four other seasons in which they lost just once. None of those great seasons resulted in a championship, though.

That is what made 2010 so special for Auburn. Newton won the school's third Heisman Trophy. And as a team, the Tigers finished with a school-record 14 wins and zero losses. Along the way, the Tigers defeated some of the best teams in the country. This time, nobody was better than Auburn.

Practically nobody saw the season coming. Auburn had lost five games in 2009. Although most expected the Tigers to be good in 2010, few expected them to be great. Auburn came into the season ranked number 22 in the Associated Press (AP) Poll. The AP Poll is one of two major polls in college football. But it was not long before the Tigers proved that ranking was too low.

Auburn won its first three games to move up to number 17 in the rankings.

## CAM'S THE MAN

Cameron "Cam" Newton played just one season at Auburn. But it was one of the greatest seasons in college football history. Newton spent his first two college seasons at the University of Florida. Then he transferred to Blinn College in Texas. He led Blinn to the national junior college championship in 2009. After that, he landed at Auburn for the 2010 season.

As the Tigers' starting quarterback, Newton threw for 2,854 yards and 30 touchdowns. He also ran for 1,473 yards and 20 touchdowns. At the end of the season, Newton easily won the Heisman Trophy voting.

"What God has blessed Cameron with is the ability to be really, really good at both [running and passing]," Auburn coach Gene Chizik said. Newton left Auburn after one season and was the first pick in the 2011 National Football League (NFL) Draft, by the Carolina Panthers.

[ 7 ]

# TIGERS

The Tigers' fourth game was against number 12 South Carolina. Auburn passed that test, too. Then the Tigers defeated Louisiana-Monroe and Kentucky. A rout over number 12 Arkansas and a win over sixth-ranked Louisiana State University (LSU) put the Tigers in the national title picture at number three. Two more wins—against Mississippi and Tennessee-Chattanooga—moved the Tigers to number two.

The Tigers' title path continued with a win against Georgia. Then, Auburn beat its biggest rival—number nine Alabama, the defending national champion.

Newton shined in the Southeastern Conference (SEC) Championship Game against number 18 South Carolina. He threw four touchdown passes and ran for two more touchdowns in the 56–17 blowout win. That win put the undefeated Tigers into the BCS title game.

"It's not even sunk in," Newton said after that win. "I've just been living the dream."

## FAIRLEY GREAT

Auburn's 2010 championship team will always be known for its offense. But the Tigers might have had the best defensive player in the country that year, too. Defensive tackle Nick Fairley was a destructive force. He finished with 60 tackles, 24 of which were for negative yards. Fairley also had 11 1/2 quarterback sacks. He won the Lombardi Award, which goes to the top lineman or linebacker in the country. Fairley was then selected thirteenth overall by the Detroit Lions in the 2011 NFL Draft.

Auburn defensive tackle Nick Fairley crushes Oregon's quarterback during the 2011 BCS title game.

Of course, the dream would get better. Just like the other 13 games that season, the Tigers walked off the field with a win over Oregon. Only this time, they carried a national championship trophy with them.

Considering where they started the year, it was a fairy tale finish. The Tigers became the first team in 20 years to start the season outside of the top 20 and then finish as national champion.

"Anything is possible," Newton said after beating Oregon. "I guarantee five or six months ago, that no one would bet their last dollar that Auburn would win the national championship. And now we're standing here."

Auburn University was originally known as Agricultural and Mechanical College of Alabama.

# EARLY YEARS

A UBURN'S FIRST-EVER FOOTBALL GAME WAS A WIN AGAINST GEORGIA ON FEBRUARY 20, 1892. THE SCHOOL, ORIGINALLY KNOWN AS AGRICULTURAL AND MECHANICAL COLLEGE OF ALABAMA, CONTINUED TO HAVE SUCCESS IN ITS EARLY YEARS.

One of the greatest runs of success in Auburn football history came under the direction of coach Mike Donahue. Donahue coached the Tigers from 1904 to 1906 and again from 1908 to 1922. He had great success throughout his entire tenure at Auburn. His overall record with the Tigers was 99–35–5. Through 2011, that was tied for the second-most wins of any coach in school history. Donahue was inducted into the College Football Hall of Fame in 1951.

Donahue's time as coach included a 23-game unbeaten streak. That remained the second-longest streak in school history through 2011. The streak began with a 53–0 win over Mercer College on October 4, 1913. And it ended when

# TIGERS

Vanderbilt defeated the Tigers 17–0 on November 13, 1915. Auburn was nearly untouchable during that 23-game streak. The Tigers allowed a total of just 13 points in those games. In fact, in 21 of those games, Auburn's opponents did not score a single point. In 1913, the Tigers finished the season 8–0. They outscored their opponents 223–13.

Even so, the 1914 squad might have been the most dominant in school history. That season, the Tigers won eight games and tied another. Most impressive was that the team did not give up a single point all season. The Tigers outscored their nine opponents 193–0.

The 1914 season included an impressive 14–0 win against a good Georgia Tech team. In that game, all-conference end Richard Kearley played a starring role.

"True, the backs did the hammering that brought the touchdowns, but it was Kearley that gave them the opportunity that they grasped,"

## TIGERS AND DOGS

Auburn's oldest rival on the football field is Georgia. In fact, Auburn-Georgia is the oldest rivalry in the Deep South. The first game between the two schools was actually Auburn's first-ever football game. It took place on February 20, 1892, at Piedmont Park in Atlanta. Frank Lupton scored Auburn's first-ever touchdown in that 10–0 win. Since 1898, the two teams have played each other in all but three years. They missed 1917 and 1918 because of World War I. They also missed 1943, when Auburn did not field a team because of World War II. Through 2011, Auburn's record against Georgia was 54–53–8.

[ 12 ]

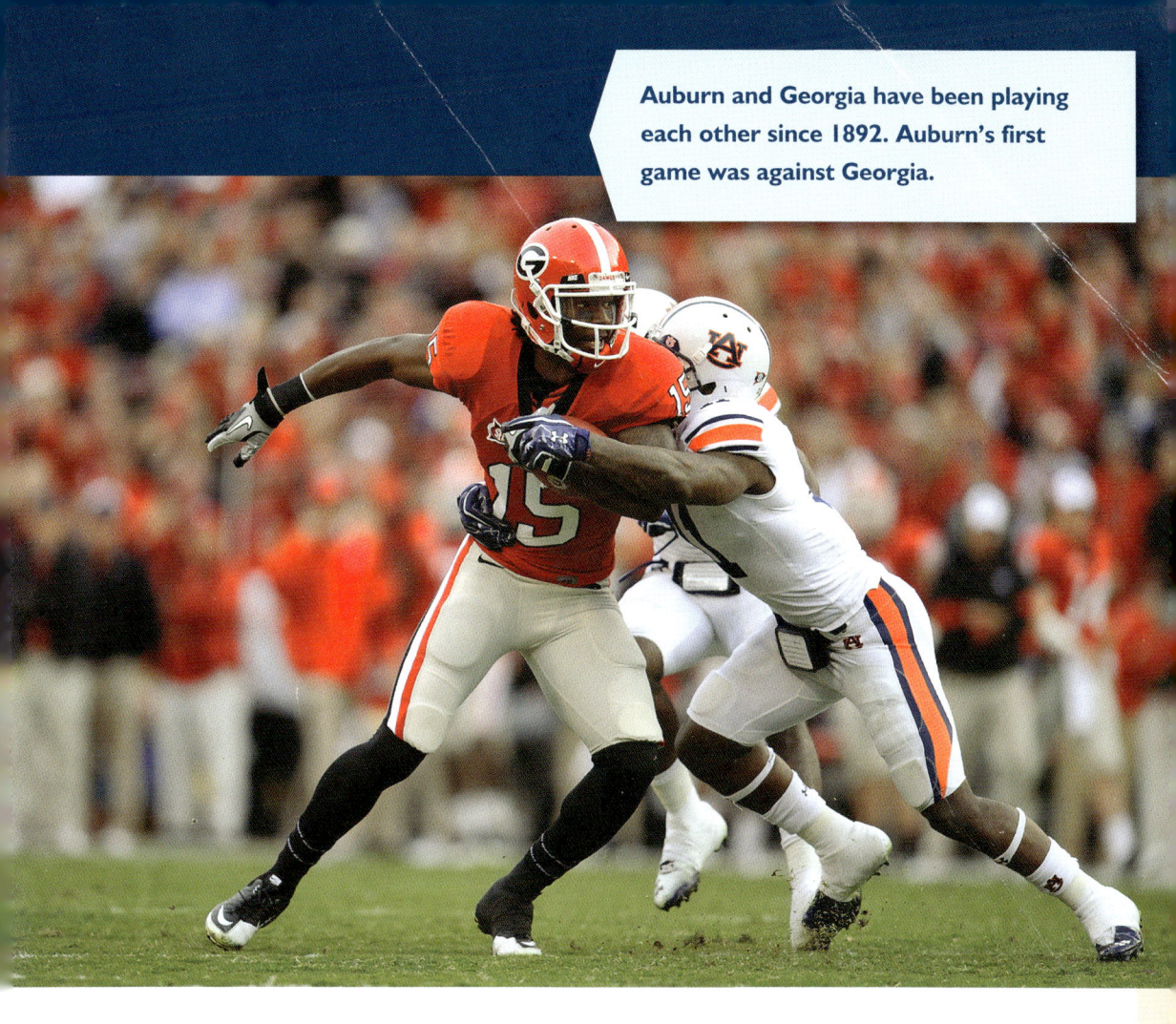

> Auburn and Georgia have been playing each other since 1892. Auburn's first game was against Georgia.

said a newspaper article the next day. "It was Kearley that recovered every one of the three Tech fumbles. He had his eyes open to every possibility. He followed the ball relentlessly and whenever it got loose [he] pounced on it like a cat."

Stars such as Kearley, Henry Robinson, and Boozer Pitts led the Tigers. They were so good in 1914 that fans of the opposing teams expected to lose. Georgia was the Tigers' main rival at the time. Prior to their game on November 21, 1914, Georgia simply hoped to score.

# TIGERS

## WAR EAGLE

Although Auburn's nickname is the Tigers, their battle cry is "War Eagle." According to Auburn legend, the cry dates back to the Civil War. The story goes that an Auburn student was fighting in the war when he was wounded and left for dead. All he could see was himself and a wounded baby eagle.

The soldier survived and nursed the wounded eagle back to health. For years, the two stayed together. The soldier eventually became a member of Auburn's faculty. On the day of Auburn's first football game against Georgia on February 20, 1892, the soldier and eagle were there. The eagle flew into the air after Auburn scored a touchdown. Auburn fans noticed the bird and shouted, "War Eagle!" The eagle, according to the story, died after the game. The battle cry, however, lives on today.

"The question of whether or not Georgia will score is the absorbing topic in advance of the game," wrote Dick Jemison of the *Atlanta Constitution*. "Even the most optimistic Georgia rooters concede the victory to Auburn, but they do not concede a shut out. A score for the Red and Black [Georgia] in this game would be a wonderful thing. They will, if they score, accomplish something that no other team has been able to accomplish this season. And Georgia is going to try her best."

Georgia did not score. But the Bulldogs did not lose, either. In fact, that was the only game in Auburn's 23-game streak that the Tigers did not win. It ended in a 0–0 tie. Georgia threatened to score three times. The *Atlanta Constitution* declared the result a "moral victory" for the Bulldogs.

Auburn won seven more games in a row after that. The Tigers took their win streak deep into the 1915 season. It was then, however, that they ran up against

Nova, Auburn's latest bald eagle, lands at the school's Jordan-Hare Stadium before a 2011 game.

Vanderbilt. Even in the loss to Vanderbilt, the Tigers were praised. A newspaper account the next day said, "Vanderbilt outplayed Auburn in every way, but Auburn fought doggedly throughout."

Football was very different at the time. It was not as popular as it is today. And some of the game play more closely resembled today's rugby than today's football. But the decade from 1910 to 1919 remains perhaps the greatest decade in Auburn history. The Tigers won 77.5 percent of their games in that decade.

The 1920s started off well, too. From 1920 to 1922, the Tigers went 20–7. Auburn dominated many of those games. They won by such scores as 88–0, 77–0, 72–0, and 61–0.

# TIGERS

Donahue announced that he was leaving Auburn during the 1922 season. He later changed his mind and said he would stay. But then, he again changed his mind. After that season, he left Auburn for LSU. It was a big loss for Auburn. In addition to his role as football coach, Donahue also coached basketball, baseball, and track and field at Auburn. He served as the school's athletic director as well.

Auburn struggled after Donahue left. Even with its success from 1920 to 1922, Auburn ended the decade with a losing record. Through 2011, it remained one of just two losing decades in Auburn's history. Four different men took their turns as head coach during that time.

Chet Wynne was hired before the 1930 season. And Auburn's fortunes finally changed. The Tigers were back to winning by 1931. In 1932, they went undefeated at 9–0–1. The Tigers also won the Southern Conference championship.

The 1932 season was a milestone year for the Tigers. Senior halfback Jimmy Hitchcock was the first player in school history to earn

## EARLY SUCCESS

Auburn was originally called Agricultural and Mechanical College of Alabama. And from the beginning, the school often had a winning football team. One of the most successful coaches was John Heisman, for whom the Heisman Trophy is named. Heisman had a 12–4–2 record as Auburn's coach from 1895 to 1899. In 1894, Auburn joined the Southern Intercollegiate Athletic Association and won three conference titles. In 1921, the Tigers became members of the Southern Conference. They won the Southern title in 1932.

> Auburn was one of the founding members of the SEC following the 1932 football season.

All-America honors that season. Hitchcock was from Union Springs, Alabama. In fact, his nickname was the "Phantom of Union Springs." He was skilled as a passer, runner, and punter. He also scored two touchdowns on defense in a game against Tulane that season.

In addition to football, Hitchcock was an All-American baseball player and played briefly in the major leagues. Auburn's baseball stadium is named after Hitchcock and his brother Billy. It is called Hitchcock Field at Plainsman Park. Billy was also a baseball standout at Auburn and later played nine seasons in the major leagues.

The SEC was formed following the 1932 season. Auburn was one of its first members. The conference change marked the beginning of a new era in Auburn Tigers football.

EARLY YEARS

An Auburn running back finds an opening against Michigan State during the Orange Bowl following the 1937 season.

# NATIONAL CHAMPS

**C**OACH CHET WYNNE GUIDED AUBURN INTO THE SEC ERA IN 1933. AFTER ONE YEAR, THOUGH, JACK MEAGHER REPLACED HIM AS HEAD COACH. FOR NINE YEARS, MEAGHER LED THE TIGERS. ALTHOUGH THEY DID NOT WIN ANY SEC TITLES DURING THAT TIME, THEY DID ENJOY SUCCESS. MEAGHER'S TEAMS HAD A RECORD OF 48–37–10.

Those years produced some of Auburn's greatest players. Offensive lineman Walker Gilbert is the only Tiger to ever be named an All-American three times, from 1934 to 1936. He also played linebacker on defense. Gilbert was later inducted into the College Football Hall of Fame.

Another Auburn great was Monk Gafford. He was named the SEC Player of the Year in 1942. He starred at running back, punter, and on defense.

The Meagher era was significant for another reason as well. Auburn played its first two postseason bowl games

> **INTERNATIONAL FLAVOR**
>
> On January 1, 1937, Auburn and Villanova played to a 7–7 tie in the Bacardi Bowl. It was the first bowl game ever played outside of the United States. The teams were lucky the game was played. It was nearly canceled when a photo of Cuban dictator Fulgencio Batista was not in the game program. The program was fixed just in time, however. Approximately 12,000 fans attended the game.

under Meagher. Teams that have won a certain amount of the regular-season games are invited to bowl games as a reward. The Tigers concluded the 1936 season with a 7–7 tie against Villanova in the Bacardi Bowl. It was played January 1, 1937, in Havana, Cuba.

Auburn wrapped up the 1937 season with a 6–0 win against Michigan State in the Orange Bowl. The Orange Bowl, played in Miami, Florida, remains one of the most prestigious bowl games.

Meagher coached the Tigers through 1942. Auburn did not field a team in 1943 because of World War II. Following the war, it took a while for the Tigers to again find their winning ways. From 1944 to 1950, they had a record of just 18–44–4. That included a 0–10 season in 1950.

But then, Ralph "Shug" Jordan took over as head coach in 1951, and the Tigers soon reached a new level of success. Jordan coached the team for 25 years. He finished with a 176–83–6 record. He is, by far, the winningest coach in Auburn history. Jordan guided the Tigers to 12 bowl games, including seven straight from 1968 to 1974. He was later named to the College Football Hall of Fame in 1982.

Jordan's best team was the 1957 squad. That season, the Tigers finished 10–0 to claim their first-ever national championship. No team scored more than seven points against the Auburn defense that season. In fact, opponents scored just 28 points against Auburn all year. The Tigers won the title despite playing just three games all season at their home stadium.

Jimmy Phillips was Auburn's only All-American in 1957. He had a brilliant season. Phillips averaged 23.8 yards per catch. End Jerry Wilson also had a great year, earning All-SEC honors. They were not the only talented players on that team, though. In all, 18 players from the 1957 squad were selected in the NFL Draft.

There was not much focus on the national title, though. In fact, it was not until the end of the season that the Tigers realized it was a possibility. There was no national championship game at the time, so voters in various polls determined the champion. The AP Poll and Coaches' Poll are considered the most important.

### ZEKE MAKES AN IMPACT

Roger Duane "Zeke" Smith came from a small town called Uniontown, Alabama. He did not get much attention as a high school player. In fact, Auburn was the only school that approached him about playing in college. He accepted and soon became a star.

A 6-foot-2, 215-pound lineman, Smith won the Outland Trophy in 1958. It is given to the country's top lineman. Smith later went on to a professional career. Auburn has given out the Zeke Smith Award to the team's top defensive player every year since 1977.

# TIGERS

## SULLIVAN TAKES THE HEISMAN

Pat Sullivan, a three-year starter at quarterback, led the country with 2,856 yards of total offense in 1970. In 1971, he became the first Auburn player to win the Heisman Trophy. That season, he threw for 2,012 yards and 20 touchdowns and ran for two touchdowns. He was named SEC Player of the Year in 1970 and 1971. In 1991, he was inducted into the College Football Hall of Fame.

"He does more things to beat you than any quarterback I've ever seen," former Alabama coach Paul "Bear" Bryant once said of Sullivan.

Sullivan's top receiver was Terry Beasley. Beasley was an All-American in 1970 and 1971. Beasley finished his career with 2,507 receiving yards. He joined Sullivan in the College Football Hall of Fame in 2002.

---

"We had gradually moved up in the polls," quarterback Lloyd Nix said years later. "The only time I ever remember coach Jordan mentioning we had a chance to win the national championship [was] when we started on the field before the Alabama game and he just said, 'Guys, if y'all have a good game, you have a chance of being a national champion.'"

Alabama did not have a good team that year, finishing just 2–7–1. The Crimson Tide were no match for the Tigers. Auburn rolled to a 40–0 win.

"That Auburn team is the best I've seen," Alabama coach J. B. Whitworth said after the game. "I certainly wouldn't want to play anybody any better than they are, if anybody is."

That year, there was nobody better. A National Collegiate Athletic Association (NCAA) violation meant the Tigers could not play in a bowl game. But nonetheless, the Tigers finished the season number one in the AP Poll to claim the title.

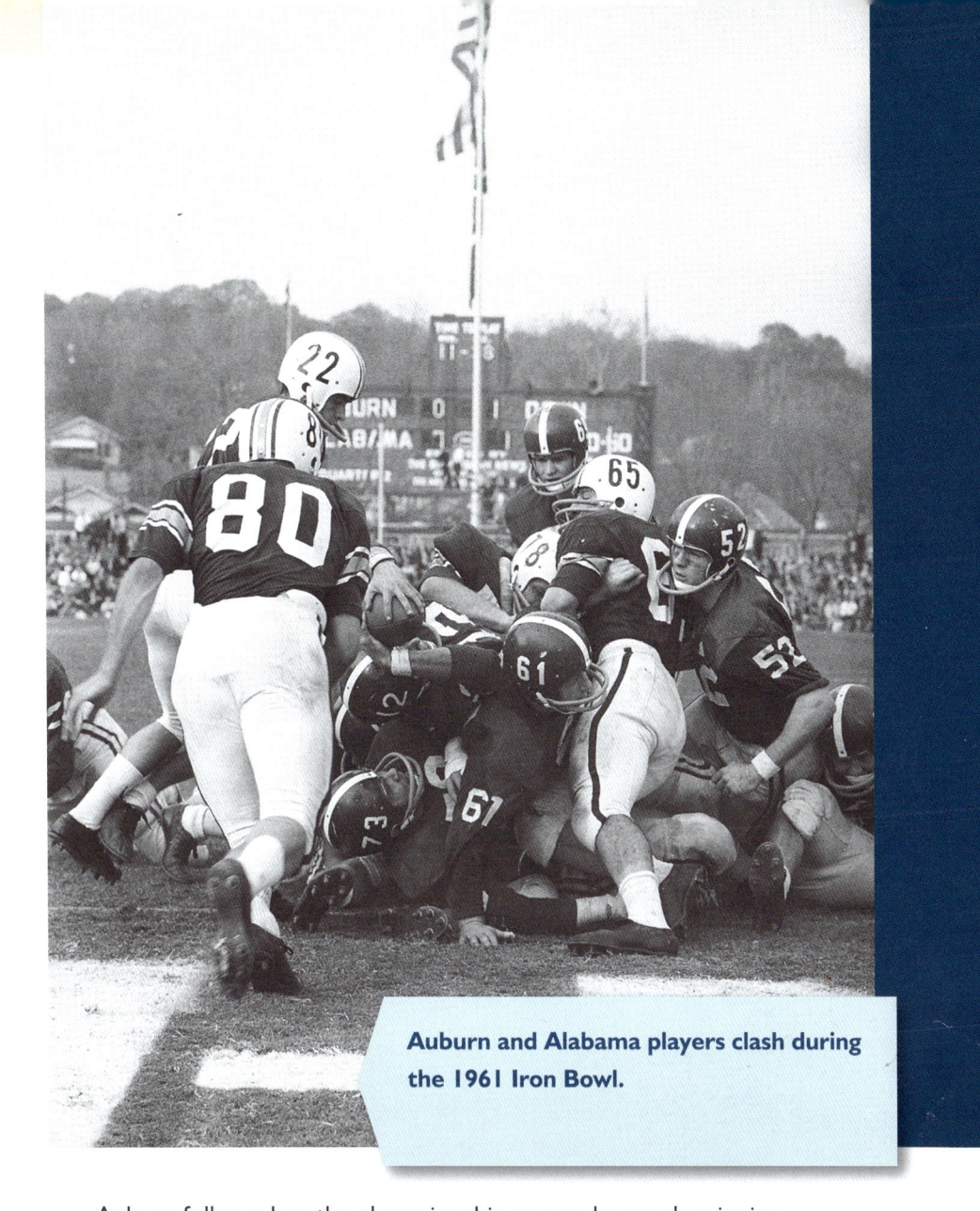

**Auburn and Alabama players clash during the 1961 Iron Bowl.**

Auburn followed up the championship season by nearly winning another in 1958. The Tigers finished 9–0–1 that season and ranked number four in the country. The only blemish on the season was a 7–7 tie against unranked Georgia Tech on October 18. Only Mississippi State scored more than eight points against the Tigers.

# TIGERS

The 1960s saw more success. In 1963, Auburn finished 9–2 and ranked fifth in the nation. Quarterback Jimmy Sidle was the SEC's Most Valuable Player. Fullback Tucker Frederickson won the award in 1964.

The Tigers came close to a title one other time during Jordan's tenure as coach. In 1972, they finished 10–1 and ranked fifth. After a 4–0 start, the Tigers traveled to Baton Rouge, Louisiana, to face LSU on October 14. Both teams were ranked in the top 10. However, LSU dominated 35–7. LSU was the only team that could stop Auburn that season. The Tigers won their last six games, including a 24–3 win over Colorado in the Gator Bowl.

Jordan coached the Tigers through 1975. He was the SEC Coach of the Year four times. And he led the Tigers to 19 winning seasons in 25 years. During his time, Jordan coached many of Auburn's all-time greats. Among them were quarterback Pat Sullivan and wide receiver Terry Beasley. Both were later inducted into the College Football Hall of Fame. Auburn's stadium, Jordan-Hare Stadium, is partially named after Jordan.

## WHAT A FINISH

Auburn and Alabama have been bitter rivals for years, and they have played some great games. One of the most famous games came in 1972. Auburn trailed 16–0 before Gardner Jett kicked a fourth-quarter field goal for the Tigers. Then came a miraculous finish. Bill Newton blocked an Alabama punt. David Langner picked it up and ran 25 yards for a touchdown. Just three minutes later, Newton blocked another punt. Langner again picked up the ball, this time going 20 yards for a touchdown. Auburn won 17–16.

**Auburn quarterback Pat Sullivan poses with the Heisman Trophy after it was awarded to him in 1971.**

Following Jordan, Doug Barfield coached the Tigers for five years. Their best season under Barfield was in 1979. They finished 8–3 and ranked sixteenth in the country. Overall, Barfield had a disappointing 29–25–1 record. But one of the best players in team history came from those years.

Running back James Brooks played for Auburn from 1977 to 1980. He had 5,596 all-purpose yards during his career. That remained a school record through 2011. And his 3,523 rushing yards remained the third most in school history.

The Barfield years were not Auburn's best. But a new era of elite play was on the horizon.

NATIONAL CHAMPS

Coach Pat Dye led Auburn to some of its greatest seasons, from 1981 to 1992.

## DYE YEARS

**P**AT DYE SEEMED TO BE AN OUTSIDER WHEN HE WAS FIRST HIRED AS AUBURN'S COACH IN JANUARY 1981. AFTER ALL, HE HAD PLAYED AT GEORGIA, WHICH WAS ONE OF AUBURN'S BIGGEST RIVALS. DYE ALSO SPENT NINE YEARS AS AN ASSISTANT AT ALABAMA, WHICH IS AUBURN'S BIGGEST RIVAL. BUT THE FORMER WYOMING COACH PUT HIS HEART INTO AUBURN.

"I am extremely happy to be back in Alabama—Auburn, Alabama, that is," he said. "I'm glad to be back in an area where football means so much to the people. People in Wyoming are talking about rodeoing in July, while people in Alabama are talking about the Alabama-Auburn game."

Dye spent 12 great years at Auburn, from 1981 to 1992. He won 99 games, which still tied for the second-most wins among Auburn coaches in 2011. Dye also won four SEC championships and led the Tigers to nine bowl games.

The Tigers struggled to a 5–6 record in Dye's first season. But they finished 9–3 and ranked fourteenth in 1982.

# TIGERS

> ## BO KNOWS RUNNING
>
> Bo Jackson was the top running back in college football in 1985. During his Heisman Trophy–winning season, he ran for at least 200 yards four times. He also scored 17 touchdowns. A few months earlier, he had a .401 batting average with 17 home runs for the Tigers' baseball team. It is not unheard-of for college athletes to play two sports. But Jackson later gained fame for playing both sports as a professional, which is uncommon.
>
> Jackson was an All-Star baseball player for the Kansas City Royals. He was also a standout running back for the NFL's Los Angeles Raiders. A major hip injury ended his football career and damaged his baseball career. But for a while, Jackson was considered one of the best athletes in the world. He even did a series of commercials in which he participated in a variety of sports, with the slogan, "Bo knows . . ."

The 1983 season was their best under Dye. That season, the Tigers went 11–1 and finished with the number-three ranking in the AP Poll. A few smaller publications even named the Tigers as national champions.

The only setback in 1983 was a 20–7 loss against Texas. After that loss, the Tigers won 10 straight games to close the season. Sophomore running back Bo Jackson had a great season in 1983. He rushed for 1,213 yards and 12 touchdowns.

As good as Jackson was in 1983, he was even better in 1985. Jackson missed half the 1984 season with an injury. He rebounded in a big way his senior year, though. That season, he rushed for 1,786 yards and 17 touchdowns. The 6-foot-1, 222-pounder from Bessemer, Alabama, took home that year's Heisman Trophy. He edged Iowa quarterback Chuck Long in what was the closest Heisman Trophy vote in history to that point.

> **Bo Jackson rushes against Texas during a 1983 game. Jackson was an all-around star athlete at Auburn.**

"It means a great deal," Jackson said after winning the award. "It's something I've looked over the years at. . . . It's a tradition I'll try to uphold."

During the 1984 and 1985 seasons, Auburn went 17–8 and played in two more bowl games. Although Jackson was gone after the 1985 season, the Tigers continued to win. From 1986 to 1989, the Tigers went 39–7–2. They finished in the top 10 of the national rankings four years in a row. And in 1989, they finished 10–2 and routed Ohio State 31–14 in the Hall of Fame Bowl.

# TIGERS

Senior quarterback Reggie Slack completed a great 1989 season with a great performance against Ohio State. He threw three touchdown passes and ran for one more.

Auburn had several All-Americans during the last half of the 1980s. Center Ben Tamburello (1985 and 1986), defensive tackle Tracy Rocker (1987 and 1988), and guard Ed King (1989 and 1990) all earned All-America honors twice. Seven other players also earned All-America honors during the late 1980s.

In 1990, the Tigers finished 8–3–1 and once again ranked among the top 20 teams in the country. They finished the season with a 27–23 win over Indiana in the Peach Bowl.

Tough times were ahead, however. From 1991 to 1992, the Tigers went a combined 10–11–1. They did not reach a bowl game in either year. Dye, who was also the athletic director, came under fire, too. Allegations of wrongdoing in the program came to light. A former player said he received illegal money benefits during his time at Auburn.

## DYE'S LEGACY

Although Pat Dye resigned as Auburn's coach during a time of turmoil, he is a beloved figure at the school. He led the Tigers to great success on the field. He also made an impact in his role as the school's athletic director. In 2005, 13 years after he finished his tenure as coach, Dye was honored by the school. The field at Jordan-Hare Stadium was named Pat Dye Field.

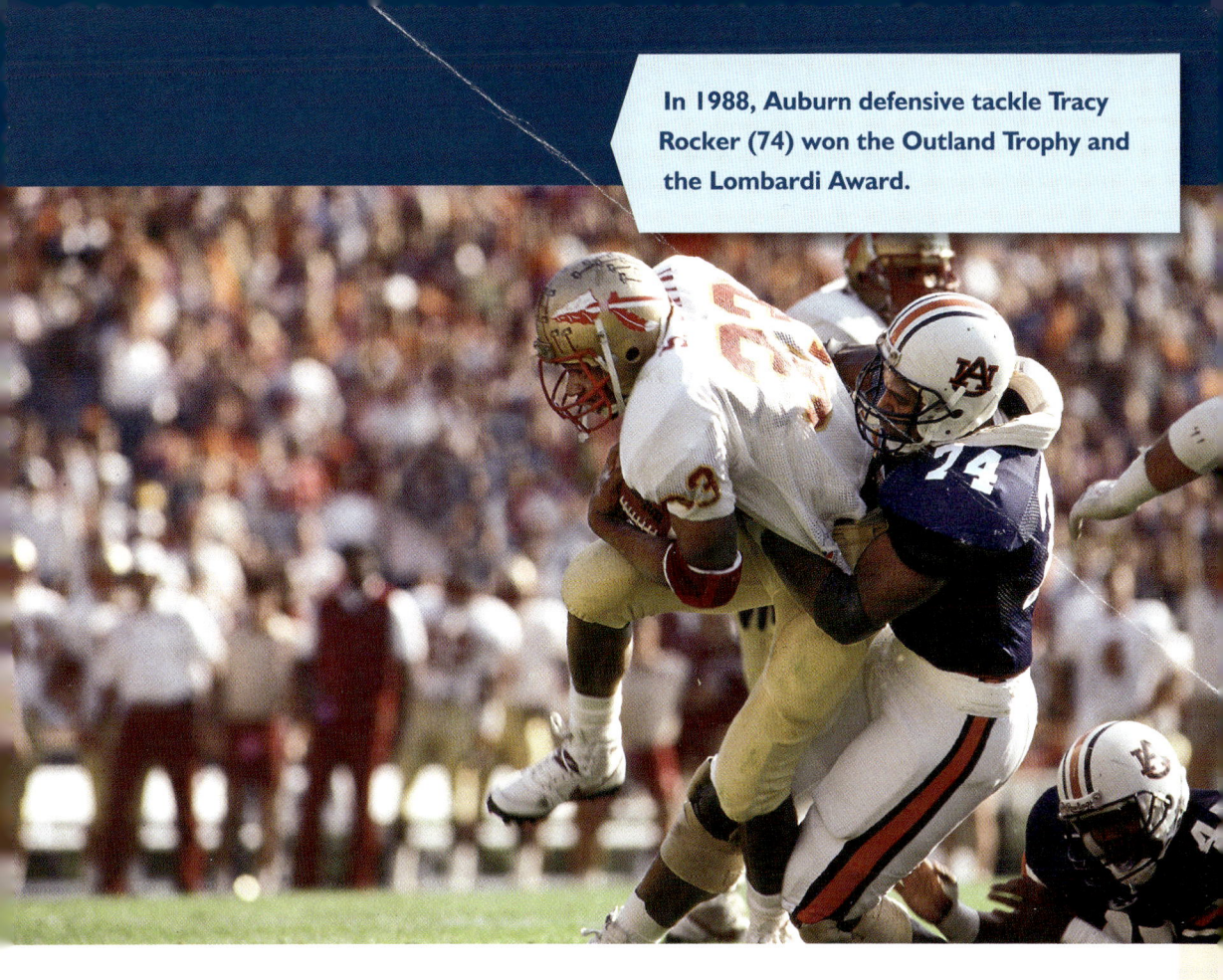

> In 1988, Auburn defensive tackle Tracy Rocker (74) won the Outland Trophy and the Lombardi Award.

Dye resigned as athletic director in 1991. Then he resigned as coach on November 25, 1992. He coached his final game—against Alabama on Thanksgiving Day—one day later.

"This is not exactly the way I would have preferred to go out," Dye said after the 17–0 loss to the Crimson Tide.

"It was tough," he said of talking to his players after the game. "We've shed enough tears in the last days to float a battleship. And I'm probably not through yet."

Although Auburn was suffering at the time, better days were ahead—and soon.

Auburn wide receiver Frank Sanders pulls down the game-winning touchdown pass in a 1994 upset over Florida.

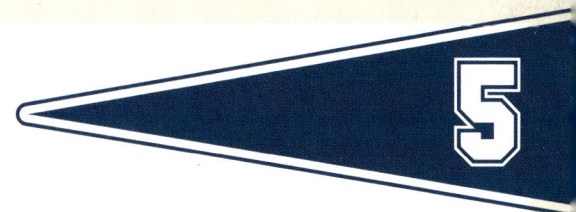

# WINNING TRADITION

**B**OBBY BOWDEN BECAME ONE OF THE MOST SUCCESSFUL COLLEGE FOOTBALL COACHES EVER WHILE AT FLORIDA STATE. HIS SON, TERRY BOWDEN, TOOK OVER AS AUBURN'S COACH BEFORE THE 1993 SEASON. BUT TERRY BOWDEN FACED CHALLENGES RIGHT FROM THE START.

The Tigers had not been a great team in the years before Bowden took over. During his first month of practice, Bowden recognized he had a tough task to change that. "We're . . . an average football team," he said. "I figure the worst thing you can call somebody is average."

Taking over a rebuilding team excited Bowden, though. "I've always been taught that if you work hard and believe in yourself, good things will happen," he said.

Bowden faced other challenges, too. Just a few weeks before Auburn's first game under Bowden, the NCAA put the team on probation. The punishment stemmed from

# TIGERS

> **CLUTCH PLAY**
>
> Auburn's undefeated season was in jeopardy during the final game of the 1993 season. The Tigers trailed Alabama 14–5 midway through the third quarter. That is when backup quarterback Patrick Nix came to the rescue. After senior starter Stan White got hurt, the sophomore Nix came in and, facing fourth-and-15, threw a 35-yard touchdown pass to junior wide receiver Frank Sanders. The play, "278Z Takeoff," is well-known among Auburn fans. The Tigers went on to win that game, 22–14.

the situation that had forced Pat Dye to resign. Probation meant the Tigers had to give away some scholarships. They also could not be on television, which limited how much money the program could make. And Auburn was ineligible for championships and bowl games for two seasons as well.

Facing all of that, Bowden and the Tigers came in to the 1993 season determined to succeed. "When coach Bowden told us this morning [about the punishments], you could see people's heads drop for just a second," senior center Greg Thompson said. "But then we said, 'No, we can't get down about this. We've got to get ready to win.'"

Few people expected Auburn to win much that first year. In fact, the Tigers began the year unranked. Yet winning was all Auburn did for a while. The Tigers surprised the college football world by going 11–0 in 1993. However, Auburn finished the season ranked number four in the AP Poll, just short of a national championship. Quarterback Stan White completed his career as Auburn's all-time leading passer.

Linebacker Takeo Spikes and coach Terry Bowden get ready to lead Auburn onto the field for a 1997 game.

The Tigers won their first nine games of 1994, stretching their win streak to 20 games. They finished that season at 9–1–1, ranked number nine. Finally, the team was off probation.

Bowden led the Tigers to a 26–11 record over the next three seasons. The Tigers went to bowl games in all three years. That included 1997, when the Tigers went 10–3, finished eleventh in the polls, and won the SEC's West Division. Auburn ended the season with a 21–17 win over Clemson in the Peach Bowl.

Bowden's future at Auburn did not last much longer, though. Just like Dye, Bowden's time at Auburn ended in a dark cloud. A series of off-the-field problems led fans to doubt whether Bowden was the right

WINNING TRADITION

[ 35 ]

# TIGERS

> **FANTASTIC FINISH**
>
> On September 17, 1994, Auburn seemed destined to lose for the first time under coach Terry Bowden. The Tigers trailed LSU 23–9 in the fourth quarter. In those final 15 minutes, however, Auburn's defense pulled off a remarkable feat. Ken Alvis, Fred Smith, and Brian Robinson all intercepted LSU passes and returned them for touchdowns. The Tigers actually intercepted five LSU passes in the fourth quarter alone and won 30–26.

man for the job. After the Tigers started the 1998 season with a 1–5 record, Bowden resigned.

"It is because of my love for these players and of Auburn University that I cannot allow this painful controversy to continue," he said on the day he resigned. "Someone must be willing to step up to the plate and put closure to this endless debate if Auburn is going to move forward. I believe that someone must now be me."

The Tigers finished the season just 3–8. The last time they finished 3–8 was in 1976, and they had not finished worse than that since 1952. Tommy Tuberville took over as coach prior to the 1999 season. Like several coaches before him, Tuberville guided the Tigers to great success. In 10 seasons, Tuberville won 85 games while losing just 40. Auburn won the SEC's West Division five times under Tuberville. The Tigers also finished ranked among the top 20 six times.

Auburn's best season with Tuberville came in 2004. That year, the Tigers went 13–0, won the SEC championship, and finished ranked second in most national rankings. By then, the BCS had been established

**Auburn running back Carnell Williams rushes past a Tennessee defender during the 2004 SEC title game.**

to pit the two top-ranked teams against each other for the national championship. Unfortunately for Auburn, the Tigers never got that chance. The BCS determined that the University of Southern California (USC) and Oklahoma were the two best teams.

Following the perfect regular season, the Tigers knocked off Virginia Tech 16–13 in the Sugar Bowl. Many voters ranked Auburn second in the final polls, ahead of Oklahoma (which had lost to USC). The debate could go on forever as to whether Auburn deserved a chance at the title. There was no debate about how Tuberville felt, however.

# TIGERS

> **ROGERS HONORED**
>
> Every year, the Jim Thorpe Trophy is awarded to the best defensive back in college football. In 2004, Carlos Rogers became the only Jim Thorpe Award winner in Auburn history. Rogers made 47 tackles and intercepted two passes that season. A standout for four years for the Tigers, Rogers was an All-American in 2004. He was the number nine choice in the 2005 NFL Draft, and as of 2011, he was still enjoying a successful pro career.

"Neither team is better than us," he said of USC and Oklahoma. "We'll play them anytime, anywhere."

Quarterback Jason Campbell certainly felt the same way. "People [don't] understand how hard it is to go 13–0," said Campbell. "I'm not going to sit here and say we're number two behind anybody."

The 2004 team was loaded with talent. Campbell had one of the best seasons of any quarterback in team history in 2004. That year's Auburn squad produced a team-record four first-round picks in the 2005 NFL Draft. They were Campbell, running backs Carnell Williams and Ronnie Brown, and cornerback Carlos Rogers.

Tuberville set the bar high during his time in Auburn. That is part of what led him out of town, though. In 2008, the Tigers stumbled to a 5–7 season. After a 3–0 start, the Tigers won just two of their last nine games. At the end of the season, Tuberville resigned amid pressure. Tuberville beat Alabama six straight times, from 2002 to 2007. That is always a big deal for any Auburn coach. But his final game as Auburn coach was a 36–0 loss to the rival Crimson Tide.

**Quarterback Jason Campbell was one of four Auburn players selected in the first round of the 2005 NFL Draft.**

Just 10 days after Tuberville left, Auburn found a new head coach. Gene Chizik was Auburn's defensive coordinator from 2002 to 2004 before leaving for jobs at Texas and Iowa State. But he returned to Alabama in December 2008 as the Tigers' new head coach.

Some doubted Chizik after his losing record at Iowa State. But he got off to a great start with the Tigers. Auburn won his first five games as Tigers' coach. And his first season, 2009, ended with an 8–5 record. That included a win over Northwestern in the Outback Bowl.

WINNING TRADITION

# TIGERS

## THE IRON BOWL

Each year, no game is bigger in the eyes of Auburn fans than the annual meeting with Alabama. Separated by just 160 miles (257 km), the two schools have met on the football field 76 times through 2011, with Alabama holding a 41–34–1 edge.

"It's the biggest day of the year, if you live in Alabama," Auburn quarterback Clint Moseley said before the 2011 contest. "I mean, you have Christmas and everything, but this is the day that everybody—people who don't even like football watch this game."

The rivalry game, known as the Iron Bowl, is one of the biggest in college football. It often impacts the national title race. In 2010, Auburn was propelled into the national title game by beating Alabama. And in 2011, Alabama secured a national title game spot by beating the Tigers.

In his second season, Chizik brought in junior college quarterback Cam Newton. He was better than anyone could have predicted. Newton, along with defensive tackle Nick Fairley, led Auburn to a 14–0 record. Newton won the Heisman Trophy that December. Then Auburn beat Oregon in the national championship game in January to give the Tigers their first national title in 53 years.

Several key players from the championship team graduated after that year, including Newton and Fairley, but the Tigers still looked forward with excitement. "I feel really excited about not just the 2011 football season, but really just kind of where we are in the program," Chizik said before the 2011 season. "Really, really excited about it."

Without Newton and Fairley, however, the Tigers did not come close to repeating their championship season. Auburn's winning streak snapped at 17 games when they lost their third

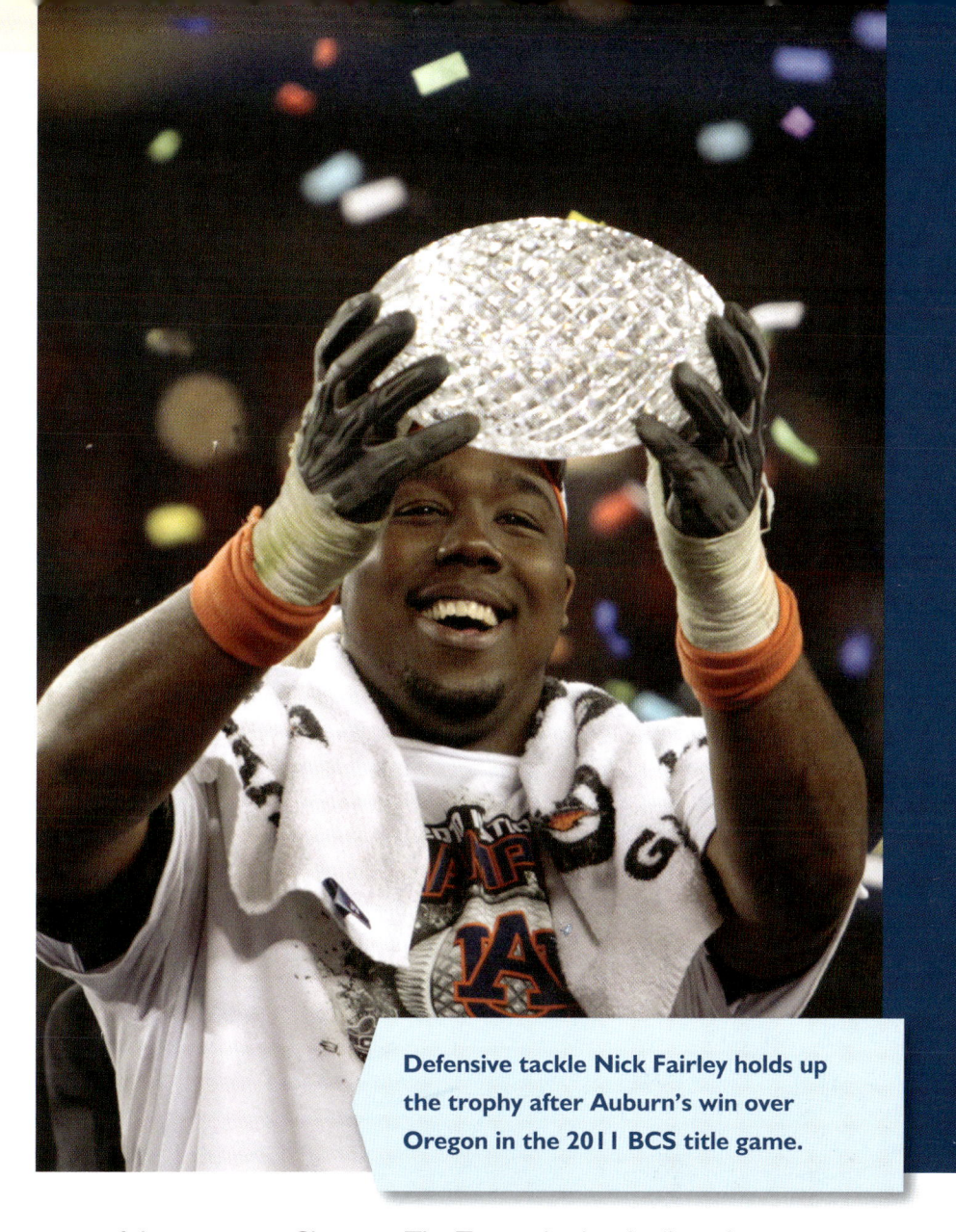

**Defensive tackle Nick Fairley holds up the trophy after Auburn's win over Oregon in the 2011 BCS title game.**

game of the season, to Clemson. The Tigers also lost badly to four top-10 teams: Arkansas, LSU, Georgia, and Alabama. With a 7–5 record, the Tigers were invited to the Chick-Fil-A Bowl.

The 2011 season did not go as well as Auburn hoped. Yet, history has proven that great seasons are never far away for the Auburn Tigers.

# TIMELINE

**1892** — Agricultural and Mechanical College of Alabama (later renamed Auburn University) plays its first football game on February 20.

**1893** — On February 22, Auburn plays—and defeats—Alabama for the first time by a score of 32–22 in Birmingham, Alabama.

**1896** — Auburn plays its first home game on November 7, defeating Georgia Tech 45–0. From 1892 to 1897, it was the only game played in Auburn.

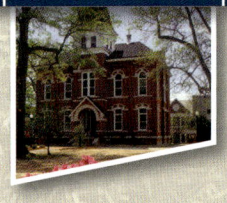

**1904** — Mike Donahue is hired as Auburn football coach. With the exception of 1907, he coached Auburn from 1904 to 1922, winning 99 games.

**1932** — Auburn (known then as Alabama Polytechnic Institute) wins its only Southern Conference championship, finishing 9–0–1.

**1971** — Quarterback Pat Sullivan becomes the first Auburn player to win the Heisman Trophy.

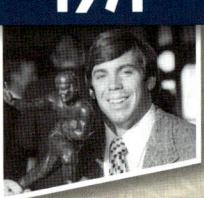

**1981** — Pat Dye is hired as Auburn coach. In 12 seasons, he won 99 games and four SEC titles.

**1983** — The Tigers finish 11–1 and third in the AP Poll. Several publications named the Tigers the national champions.

**1985** — Auburn running back Bo Jackson wins the Heisman Trophy.

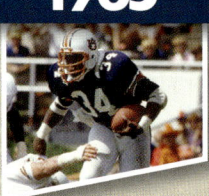

**1992** — Off the field issues lead to Dye resigning. He is replaced by Terry Bowden, son of legendary Florida State coach Bobby Bowden.

[ 42 ]

Auburn becomes one of the charter members of the SEC.

Led by third-year coach Jack Meagher, Auburn goes to a bowl game for the first time. The Tigers tied Villanova in the Bacardi Bowl in Havana, Cuba.

Because of World War II, Auburn does not field a football team.

Ralph "Shug" Jordan is hired as Auburn coach, looking to rebuild a struggling program. He would coach for 25 years, winning 176 games.

Auburn wins its first national championship. The Tigers finish 10–0 and ranked number one in the AP Poll. Then next season, they go 9–0–1, finishing a school-record streak of 24 games without a loss (23–0–1).

## 1933  1936  1943  1951  1957

Despite NCAA probation, Bowden leads Auburn to an 11–0 record and a number four national ranking. In 1994, the Tigers start 9–0, stretching their win streak to 20 games.

Struggles on and off the field lead to Bowden resigning after a 1–5 start. Before the 1999 season, Tommy Tuberville is introduced as Auburn's new coach.

Tuberville and quarterback Jason Campbell lead Auburn to a 13–0 record and the number two ranking in the final AP Poll.

Gene Chizik takes over as Auburn's twenty-sixth head coach.

Heisman Trophy–winning quarterback Cam Newton leads Auburn to its second national championship. The Tigers finish 14–0 after defeating Oregon in the BCS National Championship Game.

## 1993  1998  2004  2009  2010

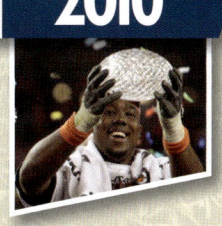

[ 43 ]

# QUICK STATS

## PROGRAM INFO
Agricultural and Mechanical College Tigers, Plainsmen (1892–98)
Alabama Polytechnic Institute Tigers, Plainsmen (1899–1959)
Auburn University Tigers (1960– )

## NATIONAL CHAMPIONSHIPS
1957, 2010

## OTHER ACHIEVEMENTS
BCS bowl appearances (1999– ): 2
SEC championships (1933– ): 7
Bowl record: 22–13–2

## HEISMAN TROPHY WINNERS
Pat Sullivan, 1971
Bo Jackson, 1985
Cam Newton, 2010

## KEY PLAYERS
(POSITION[S]; SEASONS WITH TEAM)
Terry Beasley (WR; 1969–71)
Nick Fairley (DT; 2009–10)
Tucker Frederickson (HB; 1962–64)
Walter Gilbert (G; 1934–36)
Jimmy Hitchcock (E; 1930–32)
Bo Jackson (RB; 1982–85)
Cam Newton (QB; 2010)
Jimmy "Red" Phillips (E; 1955–57)
Tracy Rocker (DT; 1985–88)
Carlos Rogers (CB; 2001–04)
Zeke Smith (G/LB; 1957–59)
Pat Sullivan (QB; 1969–71)
Stan White (QB; 1990–93)

## KEY COACHES
Mike Donahue (1904–06, 1908–22): 99–35–5
Pat Dye (1981–92): 99–39–4; 6–2–1 (bowl games)
Ralph "Shug" Jordan (1951–75): 176–83–6; 5–7 (bowl games)

## HOME STADIUM
Jordan-Hare Stadium (1939– )

* All statistics through 2011 season

# QUOTES & ANECDOTES

By 1989, it had been 96 years since rivals Auburn and Alabama first met on the football field. And they had met 53 times already. But Alabama had never played a game at Auburn's campus. Auburn had played on Alabama's campus in 1895 and 1901. But from 1902 to 1988, they had met 47 times on a neutral field in Birmingham, Alabama. The Crimson Tide visited Auburn for the first time on December 2, 1989. Since 1999, the two teams have taken turns visiting each other's campus for the annual rivalry.

"There is always this Auburn spirit you carry with you throughout your life." —Vince Dooley, Auburn quarterback, 1951 to 1953. He later became the coach at rival Georgia.

Two hours before every home game, Auburn has a tradition called "Tiger Walk." Starting in the 1960s, Tiger Walk is when the team walks from Sewell Hall to the stadium, as fans stand along Donahue Drive and cheer them on.

Toomer's Corner is an area of town where celebrations of Auburn athletics have taken place for years. After wins by the football team, Tigers fans will cover the trees at Toomer's Corner with toilet paper. Sometimes, the celebrations can last for hours. In early 2011, an Alabama fan was arrested and charged with poisoning the trees at Toomer's Corner.

# GLOSSARY

**All-American**
A player chosen as one of the best amateurs in the country in a particular activity.

**allegation**
A statement made by someone that must be proven.

**athletic director**
An administrator who oversees the coaches, players, and teams of an institution.

**conference**
In sports, a group of teams that play each other each season.

**draft**
A system used by professional sports leagues to select new players in order to spread incoming talent among all teams. The NFL Draft is held each spring.

**inducted**
To be ceremoniously admitted to a position or place, such as the hall of fame.

**ineligible**
Disqualified from playing.

**legend**
An extremely famous person, especially in a particular field.

**probation**
A period of time where a person or team tries to make up for wrongdoing.

**rankings**
A system where voters rank the best teams in the country.

**rival**
An opponent that brings out great emotion in a team, its fans, and its players.

**scholarship**
Financial assistance awarded to students to help them pay for school. Top athletes can earn a scholarship to represent a college through one of its sports teams.

**upset**
A result where the supposedly worse team defeats the supposedly better team.

# FOR MORE INFORMATION

## FURTHER READING

Glier, Ray. *What It Means to Be a Tiger.* Chicago: Triumph Books, 2010.

Housel, David. *Auburn University Football Vault: The Story of the Auburn Tigers, 1892-2007.* Atlanta, Ga.: Whitman Publishing, 2007.

Murphy, Mark. *Game of My Life: Auburn: Memorable Stories of Tigers Football.* New York: Sports Pub., 2011.

## WEB LINKS

To learn more about the Auburn Tigers, visit ABDO Publishing Company online at **www.abdopublishing.com**. Web sites about the Tigers are featured on our Book Links page. These links are routinely monitored and updated to provide the most current information available.

## PLACES TO VISIT

**College Football Hall of Fame**
111 South St. Joseph St.
South Bend, IN 46601
1-800-440-FAME (3263)
www.collegefootball.org

This hall of fame and museum highlights the greatest players and moments in the history of college football. Among the former Tigers enshrined here are Jimmy Hitchcock, Bo Jackson, and coaches Ralph "Shug" Jordan and Pat Dye.

**Jordan-Hare Stadium**
251 South Donahue Drive
Auburn, AL 36849
1-800-AUB-1957 (tickets)
www.auburntigers.com/facilities/aub-10-football.html

This has been Auburn's home field since 1939.

**Lovelace Museum**
Auburn University
Auburn, AL 36849
334-844-0764
www.auburntigers.com/facilities/aub-10-lovelace.html

This museum honors Auburn athletes through interactive exhibits.

# INDEX

Alabama, 8, 22, 24, 27, 31, 34, 38–39, 40, 41
Alvis, Ken, 36

Barfield, Doug (coach), 25
BCS National Championship Game, 5–6, 8–9, 40
Beasley, Terry, 22, 24
Bowden, Terry (coach), 33–36
Brooks, James, 25
Brown, Ronnie, 38
Byrum, Wes, 6

Campbell, Jason, 38
Chizik, Gene (coach), 7, 39–40
College Football Hall of Fame, 11, 19, 21, 22, 24

Donahue, Mike (coach), 11, 16
Dye, Pat (coach), 27–28, 30–31, 34–35
Dyer, Michael, 5–6

Fairley, Nick, 8, 40

Gafford, Monk, 19
Georgia, 8, 11, 12, 13–14, 27, 41
Gilbert, Walker, 19

Heisman, John (coach), 16
Hitchcock, Jimmy, 16–17

Iron Bowl, 40

Jackson, Bo, 28–29
Jett, Gardner, 24
Jordan, Ralph "Shug" (coach), 20–21, 22, 24–25
Jordan-Hare Stadium, 24, 30

Kearley, Richard, 12–13
King, Ed, 30

Langner, David, 24

Meagher, Jack (coach), 19–20
Moseley, Clint, 40

Newton, Cam, 5–7, 8–9, 24, 40
Nix, Lloyd, 22
Nix, Patrick, 24

Orange Bowl, 20

Phillips, Jimmy, 21
Pitts, Boozer (coach), 13

Robinson, Brian, 36
Robinson, Henry, 13
Rocker, Tracy, 30
Rogers, Carlos, 38

Sanders, Frank, 34
Sidle, Jimmy, 24
Slack, Reggie, 30
Smith, Fred, 36
Smith, Roger Duane "Zeke," 21
Sugar Bowl, 37
Sullivan, Pat, 22, 24

Tamburello, Ben, 30
Thompson, Greg, 34
Tuberville, Tommy (coach), 36–39

"War Eagle," 14
White, Stan, 34
Williams, Carnell, 38
Wilson, Jerry, 21
Wynne, Chet (coach), 16, 19

## ABOUT THE AUTHOR

Brian Howell is a freelance writer based in Denver, Colorado. He has been a sports journalist for nearly 20 years, writing about high school, college, and professional athletics. In addition, he has written books about sports and history. A native of Colorado, he lives with his wife and four children in his home state.